# 50 American Ice Cream Recipes

By: Kelly Johnson

## Table of Contents

- Vanilla Bean Ice Cream
- Chocolate Fudge Ice Cream
- Strawberry Ice Cream
- Cookies and Cream
- Mint Chocolate Chip
- Rocky Road
- Butter Pecan
- Chocolate Chip Cookie Dough
- Birthday Cake Ice Cream
- Coffee Ice Cream
- Peanut Butter Cup
- Maple Walnut
- Black Cherry Ice Cream
- Pistachio Ice Cream
- Salted Caramel Ice Cream
- Neapolitan Ice Cream
- Cotton Candy Ice Cream

- S'mores Ice Cream
- Banana Pudding Ice Cream
- Apple Pie Ice Cream
- Blueberry Cheesecake Ice Cream
- Key Lime Pie Ice Cream
- Red Velvet Ice Cream
- Pumpkin Pie Ice Cream
- Mocha Almond Fudge
- Cherry Garcia
- Brownie Batter Ice Cream
- Snickerdoodle Ice Cream
- Honey Lavender Ice Cream
- Sweet Cream Ice Cream
- Bourbon Vanilla Ice Cream
- Toasted Coconut Ice Cream
- Lemon Custard Ice Cream
- Caramel Swirl Ice Cream
- Almond Joy Ice Cream
- Fudge Ripple Ice Cream

- White Chocolate Raspberry
- Graham Cracker Swirl
- Blackberry Cobbler Ice Cream
- Chocolate Marshmallow Ice Cream
- Molasses Cookie Ice Cream
- Peppermint Bark Ice Cream
- Orange Creamsicle Ice Cream
- Brown Sugar Cinnamon Ice Cream
- Cereal Milk Ice Cream
- Toffee Crunch Ice Cream
- Chocolate Peanut Butter Swirl
- Graham Cracker Ice Cream
- Buttermilk Ice Cream
- Eggnog Ice Cream

**Vanilla Bean Ice Cream**

**Ingredients:**

- 2 cups heavy cream
- 1 cup whole milk
- 3/4 cup sugar
- 1 vanilla bean (or 2 tsp vanilla extract)
- 5 large egg yolks

**Instructions:**
Split the vanilla bean and scrape seeds into a saucepan. Add pod, cream, and milk. Heat until steaming.
Whisk egg yolks with sugar. Slowly pour in hot cream, whisking constantly.
Return to saucepan and cook over low heat until thick enough to coat a spoon.
Strain, chill mixture completely, then churn in an ice cream maker.

**Chocolate Fudge Ice Cream**

**Ingredients:**

- 2 cups heavy cream
- 1 cup whole milk
- 3/4 cup sugar
- 1/2 cup unsweetened cocoa powder
- 200 g dark chocolate, chopped
- 5 egg yolks

**Instructions:**
Heat milk, sugar, and cocoa until warm. Whisk yolks separately, then temper with hot mixture.
Cook until thick, then stir in chocolate until melted.
Add cream and chill. Churn when cold for a rich, fudgy texture.

**Strawberry Ice Cream**

**Ingredients:**

- 2 cups fresh strawberries, hulled
- 3/4 cup sugar (divided)
- 2 cups heavy cream
- 1 cup whole milk
- 1 tsp lemon juice
- 5 egg yolks

**Instructions:**
Mash strawberries with 1/4 cup sugar and lemon juice. Let sit.
Make custard base with cream, milk, remaining sugar, and egg yolks.
Chill custard, then mix in strawberry puree.
Churn and freeze.

**Cookies and Cream**

**Ingredients:**

- 2 cups heavy cream
- 1 cup whole milk
- 3/4 cup sugar
- 1 tbsp vanilla extract
- 5 egg yolks
- 15 crushed chocolate sandwich cookies (e.g., Oreos)

**Instructions:**
Make vanilla custard base and chill.
Churn in an ice cream maker, then fold in cookie chunks during the last minute.
Freeze until firm.

**Mint Chocolate Chip**

**Ingredients:**

- 2 cups heavy cream
- 1 cup whole milk
- 3/4 cup sugar
- 5 egg yolks
- 1 tsp peppermint extract
- Optional: green food coloring
- 1/2 cup mini chocolate chips

**Instructions:**
Make custard base with milk, cream, yolks, and sugar.
Stir in peppermint and optional coloring. Chill, churn, and add chocolate chips toward the end.

**Rocky Road**

**Ingredients:**

- 2 cups chocolate custard base (see Chocolate Fudge Ice Cream)
- 1/2 cup mini marshmallows
- 1/3 cup chopped toasted almonds
- Optional: chocolate chunks

**Instructions:**
Churn chocolate base. Near the end, fold in marshmallows, almonds, and chocolate. Freeze until scoopable.

## Butter Pecan

### Ingredients:

- 1/2 cup chopped pecans
- 2 tbsp butter
- 2 cups heavy cream
- 1 cup whole milk
- 3/4 cup brown sugar
- 5 egg yolks
- 1 tsp vanilla

### Instructions:
Toast pecans in butter, then cool.
Make custard with brown sugar, yolks, milk, and cream.
Stir in vanilla and chill.
Churn and fold in pecans.

**Chocolate Chip Cookie Dough**

**Ingredients:**

- Vanilla ice cream base (see Vanilla Bean Ice Cream)
- 1/2 cup mini chocolate chips
- 1/2 cup edible cookie dough (flour heat-treated and no eggs)

**Instructions:**
Churn vanilla base.
Fold in small pieces of cookie dough and chocolate chips during the last minute.
Freeze until set.

**Birthday Cake Ice Cream**

**Ingredients:**

- 2 cups heavy cream
- 1 cup whole milk
- 3/4 cup sugar
- 1 tsp vanilla extract
- 1/2 cup crushed vanilla or funfetti cake pieces
- 1/4 cup rainbow sprinkles
- Optional: 1/2 tsp butter extract for cake flavor
- 5 egg yolks

**Instructions:**
Make a vanilla custard base. Chill and churn. During the last minute, fold in sprinkles and cake chunks. Freeze until firm.

**Coffee Ice Cream**

**Ingredients:**

- 2 cups heavy cream
- 1 cup whole milk
- 3/4 cup sugar
- 5 egg yolks
- 2 tbsp instant espresso powder or 1/2 cup strong brewed espresso

**Instructions:**
Make a custard base, dissolving espresso in warm milk/cream mixture. Cook until thick, then chill. Churn and freeze.

**Peanut Butter Cup Ice Cream**

**Ingredients:**

- 2 cups heavy cream
- 1 cup whole milk
- 3/4 cup sugar
- 1/2 cup smooth peanut butter
- 5 egg yolks
- 1 cup chopped peanut butter cups

**Instructions:**
 Make custard base, whisking in peanut butter until smooth. Chill, churn, and fold in candy pieces during last minute.

**Maple Walnut Ice Cream**

**Ingredients:**

- 2 cups heavy cream
- 1 cup whole milk
- 3/4 cup pure maple syrup
- 1/2 cup toasted walnuts, chopped
- 5 egg yolks

**Instructions:**

Heat cream and milk with maple syrup. Make custard base. Chill, churn, and fold in toasted walnuts before freezing.

**Black Cherry Ice Cream**

**Ingredients:**

- 2 cups heavy cream
- 1 cup whole milk
- 3/4 cup sugar
- 2 cups pitted black cherries (fresh or frozen), chopped
- 1 tsp lemon juice
- 5 egg yolks

**Instructions:**
Cook cherries with a little sugar and lemon juice until syrupy. Cool.
Make vanilla custard base, chill, churn, and swirl in cherry mixture at the end.

**Pistachio Ice Cream**

**Ingredients:**

- 2 cups heavy cream
- 1 cup whole milk
- 3/4 cup sugar
- 1/2 cup shelled unsalted pistachios, ground
- 1/4 tsp almond extract (optional)
- 5 egg yolks
- Green food coloring (optional)

**Instructions:**
Heat cream, milk, sugar, and ground pistachios. Infuse, then strain.
Whisk into yolks to make custard. Chill, churn, add extract and color if desired.

**Salted Caramel Ice Cream**

**Ingredients:**

- 1 cup sugar (for caramel)
- 2 tbsp butter
- 1/2 tsp sea salt
- 2 cups heavy cream
- 1 cup whole milk
- 5 egg yolks

**Instructions:**
Melt sugar to a deep amber. Add butter, salt, then cream slowly. Stir until smooth.
Add milk, temper into yolks, cook to thicken.
Strain, chill, churn, and freeze.

**Neapolitan Ice Cream**

**Ingredients:**

- 1 batch each of vanilla, chocolate, and strawberry ice cream bases

**Instructions:**
Churn each flavor separately. In a loaf pan, layer vanilla, chocolate, and strawberry ice creams.
Freeze until solid. Slice to serve all three flavors in one.

**Cotton Candy Ice Cream**

**Ingredients:**

- 2 cups heavy cream
- 1 cup whole milk
- 3/4 cup sugar
- 1/2 tsp cotton candy flavoring
- Pink and blue food coloring (optional)
- 5 egg yolks

**Instructions:**
Make a standard custard base. After straining, stir in cotton candy flavor and color. Churn, then swirl pink and blue together before freezing for a carnival look.

**S'mores Ice Cream**

**Ingredients:**

- 2 cups heavy cream
- 1 cup whole milk
- 3/4 cup sugar
- 5 egg yolks
- 1/2 cup crushed graham crackers
- 1/2 cup mini marshmallows
- 1/2 cup chocolate chunks or ganache

**Instructions:**
Make vanilla custard base and chill. Churn, then fold in graham crumbs, marshmallows, and chocolate at the end.

**Banana Pudding Ice Cream**

**Ingredients:**

- 2 cups heavy cream
- 1 cup whole milk
- 3/4 cup sugar
- 2 ripe bananas, mashed
- 1 tsp vanilla extract
- 5 egg yolks
- 1/2 cup vanilla wafer cookie pieces

**Instructions:**
Make custard base and mix in mashed bananas and vanilla. Churn, then add cookie pieces in the final minute.

**Apple Pie Ice Cream**

**Ingredients:**

- 2 cups heavy cream
- 1 cup whole milk
- 3/4 cup sugar
- 5 egg yolks
- 1 tsp cinnamon
- 1 cup apple pie filling (chopped apples, brown sugar, cinnamon, butter)
- 1/2 cup pie crust crumbles or graham crackers

**Instructions:**
Swirl cooled apple pie filling into churned cinnamon custard base, then fold in crust bits. Freeze.

**Blueberry Cheesecake Ice Cream**

**Ingredients:**

- 2 cups heavy cream
- 1 cup whole milk
- 3/4 cup sugar
- 4 oz cream cheese, softened
- 5 egg yolks
- 1 tsp vanilla
- 1/2 cup blueberry compote
- 1/2 cup graham cracker pieces

**Instructions:**
Blend cream cheese into custard base. Chill, churn, then swirl in blueberry compote and graham bits.

**Key Lime Pie Ice Cream**

**Ingredients:**

- 2 cups heavy cream
- 1 cup sweetened condensed milk
- 1/2 cup key lime juice
- Zest of 1 lime
- 1/2 cup graham cracker crumbs

**Instructions (no-cook style):**
Whisk all ingredients except crumbs until smooth.
Churn, then fold in crumbs at the end. Freeze until firm.

**Red Velvet Ice Cream**

**Ingredients:**

- 2 cups heavy cream
- 1 cup whole milk
- 3/4 cup sugar
- 2 tbsp cocoa powder
- 1 tsp vanilla
- 5 egg yolks
- Red food coloring
- Optional: chunks of red velvet cake or cream cheese swirl

**Instructions:**
Make a cocoa custard base, add coloring and vanilla. Chill and churn. Swirl in cake or cream cheese frosting if desired.

**Pumpkin Pie Ice Cream**

**Ingredients:**

- 2 cups heavy cream
- 1 cup whole milk
- 3/4 cup brown sugar
- 5 egg yolks
- 1 cup canned pumpkin purée
- 1 tsp pumpkin pie spice
- 1/2 tsp vanilla

**Instructions:**
Whisk pumpkin and spice into custard base after cooking. Chill, churn, and freeze.

**Mocha Almond Fudge Ice Cream**

**Ingredients:**

- 2 cups heavy cream
- 1 cup whole milk
- 3/4 cup sugar
- 2 tbsp instant espresso powder
- 1/2 cup semi-sweet chocolate chunks or fudge ripple
- 1/2 cup toasted almonds, chopped
- 5 egg yolks

**Instructions:**
Make custard base, dissolving espresso in the heated milk/cream. Chill, churn, fold in almonds and swirl in fudge at the end.

**Cherry Garcia**

**Inspired by Ben & Jerry's**
**Ingredients:**

- 2 cups heavy cream
- 1 cup whole milk
- 3/4 cup sugar
- 1 tsp vanilla extract
- 1 cup pitted, chopped cherries (fresh or frozen)
- 1/2 cup dark chocolate chunks
- 5 egg yolks

**Instructions:**
Make vanilla custard, chill, and churn. Fold in cherries and chocolate just before freezing.

**Brownie Batter Ice Cream**

**Ingredients:**

- 2 cups heavy cream
- 1 cup whole milk
- 3/4 cup sugar
- 1/3 cup cocoa powder
- 5 egg yolks
- 1/2 cup edible brownie batter or baked brownie chunks

**Instructions:**
Make chocolate custard base. Chill and churn. Fold in brownie batter or chunks at the end.

**Snickerdoodle Ice Cream**

**Ingredients:**

- 2 cups heavy cream
- 1 cup whole milk
- 3/4 cup sugar
- 1 tsp cinnamon
- 1/4 tsp nutmeg
- 1 tsp vanilla
- 1/2 cup cinnamon sugar cookie chunks
- 5 egg yolks

**Instructions:**
Make cinnamon-spiced custard base. Chill and churn. Fold in cookie chunks near the end.

**Honey Lavender Ice Cream**

**Ingredients:**

- 2 cups heavy cream
- 1 cup whole milk
- 1/2 cup honey
- 1 tbsp dried culinary lavender
- 5 egg yolks

**Instructions:**
Heat milk, cream, and lavender. Steep for 15 mins, then strain. Whisk into yolks, cook custard. Chill, churn, and freeze.

**Sweet Cream Ice Cream**

**Ingredients:**

- 2 cups heavy cream
- 1 cup whole milk
- 3/4 cup sugar
- Pinch of salt
- 1 tsp vanilla (optional)
- 5 egg yolks

**Instructions:**
Make classic custard base without added flavorings for a pure cream taste. Chill, churn, and serve as-is or pair with pies.

**Bourbon Vanilla Ice Cream**

**Ingredients:**

- 2 cups heavy cream
- 1 cup whole milk
- 3/4 cup sugar
- 1 vanilla bean or 2 tsp vanilla extract
- 1 tbsp bourbon
- 5 egg yolks

**Instructions:**
Prepare custard base with vanilla and chill. Stir in bourbon before churning.

**Toasted Coconut Ice Cream**

**Ingredients:**

- 2 cups heavy cream
- 1 cup whole milk
- 3/4 cup sugar
- 3/4 cup unsweetened shredded coconut, toasted
- 5 egg yolks

**Instructions:**

Steep toasted coconut in warm cream for 20 mins. Strain, then use cream to make custard base. Chill, churn, and add extra coconut if desired.

**Lemon Custard Ice Cream**

**Ingredients:**

- 2 cups heavy cream
- 1 cup whole milk
- 3/4 cup sugar
- Zest of 2 lemons
- 1/2 cup fresh lemon juice
- 5 egg yolks

**Instructions:**
Heat cream, milk, sugar, and zest. Temper into egg yolks, cook until thick. Cool slightly, stir in lemon juice. Chill, churn, and freeze.

**Caramel Swirl Ice Cream**

**Ingredients:**

- 2 cups heavy cream
- 1 cup whole milk
- 3/4 cup sugar
- 5 egg yolks
- 1/2 to 3/4 cup thick caramel sauce

**Instructions:**
 Make vanilla custard base. Chill and churn. In the last minute, swirl in caramel gently to create ribbons. Freeze.

**Almond Joy Ice Cream**

**Ingredients:**

- 2 cups heavy cream
- 1 cup whole milk
- 3/4 cup sugar
- 1/2 tsp almond extract
- 1/2 cup toasted coconut
- 1/2 cup chopped almonds
- 1/2 cup chopped dark chocolate
- 5 egg yolks

**Instructions:**
Make custard base with almond extract. Chill, churn, and fold in coconut, almonds, and chocolate at the end.

**Fudge Ripple Ice Cream**

**Ingredients:**

- 2 cups heavy cream
- 1 cup whole milk
- 3/4 cup sugar
- 5 egg yolks
- 1/2 cup thick fudge sauce

**Instructions:**
 Make vanilla custard base. Chill and churn. Swirl in fudge gently just before freezing to create ripples.

**White Chocolate Raspberry Ice Cream**

**Ingredients:**

- 2 cups heavy cream
- 1 cup whole milk
- 3/4 cup sugar
- 1/2 cup white chocolate, melted
- 1/2 cup raspberry jam or compote
- 5 egg yolks

**Instructions:**
Add melted white chocolate to warm custard base. Chill and churn. Swirl in raspberry jam before freezing.

**Graham Cracker Swirl Ice Cream**

**Ingredients:**

- 2 cups heavy cream
- 1 cup whole milk
- 3/4 cup sugar
- 1 tsp vanilla
- 1/2 cup crushed graham crackers
- 1/2 cup graham cracker swirl (graham crumbs + melted butter + brown sugar)
- 5 egg yolks

**Instructions:**
 Make vanilla custard base. Chill, churn, and fold in crushed grahams and swirl mix right before freezing.

**Blackberry Cobbler Ice Cream**

**Ingredients:**

- 2 cups heavy cream
- 1 cup whole milk
- 3/4 cup sugar
- 1 tsp vanilla
- 1/2 cup blackberry compote
- 1/2 cup cobbler crumble (baked streusel or biscuit pieces)
- 5 egg yolks

**Instructions:**
 Make vanilla custard. Chill, churn, and gently fold in blackberry compote and crumble at the end.

**Chocolate Marshmallow Ice Cream**

**Ingredients:**

- 2 cups heavy cream
- 1 cup whole milk
- 3/4 cup sugar
- 1/3 cup cocoa powder
- 1/2 cup marshmallow fluff or mini marshmallows
- 5 egg yolks

**Instructions:**
Make chocolate custard base. Chill and churn. Swirl in marshmallow fluff or fold in minis just before freezing.

**Molasses Cookie Ice Cream**

**Ingredients:**

- 2 cups heavy cream
- 1 cup whole milk
- 3/4 cup dark brown sugar
- 1 tbsp molasses
- 1 tsp ground ginger
- 1/2 tsp cinnamon
- 1/4 tsp nutmeg
- 5 egg yolks
- 1/2 cup molasses cookie chunks

**Instructions:**
Make custard base with spices and molasses. Chill, churn, then fold in cookie chunks before freezing.

**Peppermint Bark Ice Cream**

**Ingredients:**

- 2 cups heavy cream
- 1 cup whole milk
- 3/4 cup sugar
- 1 tsp peppermint extract
- 1/2 cup crushed peppermint candies
- 1/2 cup chopped white & dark chocolate (or actual peppermint bark)
- 5 egg yolks

**Instructions:**
Make vanilla-mint custard base. Chill and churn. Fold in candies and chocolate just before freezing.

**Orange Creamsicle Ice Cream**

**Ingredients:**

- 2 cups heavy cream
- 1 cup whole milk
- 3/4 cup sugar
- 1/2 cup orange juice (fresh or concentrate)
- 1 tsp orange zest
- 1 tsp vanilla extract
- 5 egg yolks

**Instructions:**
Make custard base with zest. Stir in orange juice and vanilla after cooling. Chill, churn, and freeze.

**Brown Sugar Cinnamon Ice Cream**

**Ingredients:**

- 2 cups heavy cream
- 1 cup whole milk
- 3/4 cup brown sugar
- 1 tsp ground cinnamon
- 1/4 tsp salt
- 5 egg yolks

**Instructions:**
Make custard base using brown sugar and cinnamon. Chill, churn, and enjoy as a cozy, caramelized flavor on its own or paired with pies.

**Cereal Milk Ice Cream**

**Ingredients:**

- 2 cups heavy cream
- 1 cup whole milk
- 2 cups sweet cereal (like Cornflakes or Fruity Pebbles)
- 3/4 cup sugar
- 5 egg yolks

**Instructions:**
Soak cereal in warm milk/cream for 20 mins. Strain and press out liquid. Use infused milk to make custard. Chill, churn, and freeze.

**Toffee Crunch Ice Cream**

**Ingredients:**

- 2 cups heavy cream
- 1 cup whole milk
- 3/4 cup sugar
- 1 tsp vanilla extract
- 5 egg yolks
- 1/2 cup crushed toffee bits (like Heath or Skor bars)

**Instructions:**
 Make a standard vanilla custard base. Chill and churn. Fold in toffee bits at the end for crunch and caramel flavor.

**Chocolate Peanut Butter Swirl**

**Ingredients:**

- 2 cups heavy cream
- 1 cup whole milk
- 3/4 cup sugar
- 1/3 cup cocoa powder
- 5 egg yolks
- 1/2 cup peanut butter, melted

**Instructions:**
Prepare chocolate custard base. Chill and churn. Swirl in melted peanut butter during the last minute of churning or when transferring to a container.

**Graham Cracker Ice Cream**

**Ingredients:**

- 2 cups heavy cream
- 1 cup whole milk
- 3/4 cup sugar
- 1 tsp vanilla extract
- 1/2 tsp cinnamon (optional)
- 5 egg yolks
- 1/2 cup crushed graham crackers

**Instructions:**
Make vanilla custard base. Chill and churn. Fold in graham cracker crumbs just before freezing for a creamy s'mores-like effect.

## Buttermilk Ice Cream

**Ingredients:**

- 1 cup heavy cream
- 1 cup whole milk
- 3/4 cup sugar
- 1 cup buttermilk
- 1 tsp vanilla
- 5 egg yolks

**Instructions:**
Make a custard base with cream and milk. After cooling, stir in buttermilk and vanilla. Chill, churn, and enjoy a tangy, creamy ice cream.

---

## Eggnog Ice Cream

**Ingredients:**

- 2 cups heavy cream
- 1 cup whole milk
- 3/4 cup sugar
- 1/2 tsp nutmeg
- 1/4 tsp cinnamon
- 1 tsp vanilla

- 1–2 tbsp bourbon or rum (optional)
- 5 egg yolks

**Instructions:**
 Make a spiced custard base. Chill and churn. Add liquor just before churning if using for an authentic holiday kick.